Dulce et Decorum est

Wilfred Owen

Dulce et Decorum Est

Illustrated by
Martin Impey

Foreword by Jane Potter

STRAUSS HOUSE
PRODUCTIONS

for
Charlie & Molly

first printed October 2018

STRAUSS HOUSE PRODUCTIONS
www.strausshouseproductions.com

First published in Great Britain 2018
Text by Wilfred Owen
Foreword copyright © Jane Potter 2018
Illustrations copyright © Martin Impey 2018
Martin Impey has asserted his rights
to be identified as the illustrator of this work under
The Copyright, Designs and Patents Act, 1988
British Library Cataloguing in Publication Data
A catalogue record for this book is available from the British Library
All rights reserved. ISBN - 978-1-5272-1825-3
Printed in the UK

Foreword

In October 1917, whilst recovering from shell-shock at Craiglockhart War Hospital in Edinburgh, Wilfred Owen wrote to his mother Susan:

Here is a gas poem, done yesterday, (which is not private, but not final). The famous Latin tag means of course It is sweet and meet to die for one's country. Sweet! *And* decorous!

The gas poem is 'Dulce et Decorum Est', imagined in the pages that follow through the haunting illustrations of Martin Impey. It is a poem of both protest and pity: protest against those who would send young men to their deaths in war, blithely declaring platitudes such as that from Horace's Odes, or *'The old Lie'*, as Owen called it, and pity for those same young men who faced the horrors of war. The poem calls for pity not just for the solider who suffers an excruciating death by gas, but for the speaker of the poem who relives the harrowing event in his *'smothering dreams'* ever after. 'Dulce et Decorum Est' is perhaps Owen's most fierce poem and it is the power of his words that make it so.

Wilfred Edward Salter Owen was born on 18 March 1893 at Plas Wilmot, Oswestry, the home of his maternal grandfather Edward Shaw. He was the first of the four children of Tom and Susan Owen. His siblings were Mary (born 1896), Harold (born 1897) and Colin (born 1900). The death of Edward Shaw revealed such debts that

Plas Wilmot had to be sold and the family moved first, to Shrewsbury then to Birkenhead, where Tom was a railway stationmaster. They settled back in Shrewsbury when Tom became an assistant superintendent of the Joint Railways. Wilfred Owen was his mother's favourite child, her *'precious boy'* as she called him, and throughout his life, he maintained an extremely strong bond with her, a bond revealed in the letters he wrote to her: over 550 of the more than 670 letters in Owen's archive are addressed to her.

An avid reader and devotee of poetry from a young age, Wilfred Owen was educated at the Birkenhead Institute and at Shrewsbury Technical School. He hoped to go to university, but having failed to win a scholarship, he took up a post as a lay assistant to the vicar of Dunsden near Reading in 1911. He was working as an English tutor in France when the War began in 1914.

Initially, the outbreak of hostilities bothered Owen *'less than it ought'*, as he wrote to his mother, but his attitude changed, and he found himself *'intensely'* wanting *'to fight'*. In October 1915, Owen enlisted in the Artists' Rifles, was commissioned second lieutenant in the Manchester Regiment in 1916, and trained in London and the north of England before embarking for active service in January 1917. The *'fine heroic feeling'* he had on arrival in France, quickly turned into *'the Real Thing'* as Owen experienced battle on the Western Front. In April 1917, in the line at Savy Wood, Owen was blown into the air and landed in a railway embankment. He described to his mother how he:

passed most of the following days in a railway Cutting, in a hole just big enough to lie in, and covered with corrugated iron.

He lay for several days next to a dead, *'brother officer'*. As he wrote to his sister Mary:

You know it was not the Bosche that worked me up, nor the explosives, but it was living so long by poor old Cock Robin (as we used to call 2/Lt. Gaukroger), who lay not only near by, but in various places around and about, if you understand. I hope you don't!

Diagnosed with neurasthenia or shell-shock, Owen was sent back to England where, at the Welsh Hospital Netley (the Royal Victoria Hospital) at Southampton Water, a Medical Board marked him unfit for general service for six months, and posted him to Craiglockhart War Hospital in Edinburgh. Here he met Siegfried Sassoon, one of the most crucial events of his lifetime and one of the most famous encounters in literary history. Under the older poet's tutelage, Owen honed his poetic skills, and under the care of Dr Arthur Brock RAMC, Owen learned how to channel his horrific memories of battle, which he relived in his *'smothering dreams'*, into poems such as 'Dulce et Decorum Est'.

Filled with the language and imagery of Owen's most profound literary influences, the Bible, the Romantic poets Keats and Shelley, and the French poets he studied in

France before the War, 'Dulce et Decorum Est' also features a new language, a language of trenches. The poem is perhaps one of the supreme examples of Owen's mastery of these influences.

The earliest surviving manuscript is dated *'Oct. 8, 1917'* and was drafted at Craiglockhart. Owen's letters are a key source for the poem's origins. In January 1917, after his first experience of battle, he wrote to his mother of:

> *craters full of water. Men have been known to drown in them. Many stuck in the mud.*

In another letter described a gas attack in which the word *'gas'* is set out in capital letters, just as it is in the poem:

> *I went on ahead to scout – foolishly alone – and when, half a mile away from the party, got overtaken by GAS.*

In this letter Owen is describing tear gas, but in the poem, the gas is chlorine, source of the *'thick green light'* and the *'green sea'*, which when inhaled, destroys the lungs, causing the victim to drown, *'guttering, choking'*. The soldier, *'the someone'* who is *'yelling out and stumbling'*, is unable to put on his protective mask, a *'clumsy helmet'* with its celluloid windows for the eyes, which are *'the misty panes'* through which the speaker sees the frightful, gruesome event.

The *'friend'*, the *'you'* to whom the final lines are addressed is, we know from Owen's manuscripts, the humorous versifier and author Jessie Pope. Pope's patriotic, enthusiastic, and satiric poems were frequently published in *The Daily Mail* and *Punch*, and in volumes such as *Jessie Pope's War Poems* (1915) and *Simple Rhymes for Stirring Times* (1916). Owen's first draft of the poem has the dedication *'To Jessie Pope, etc'*, then in a subsequent version, *'To a Certain Poetess'*, a label suggested by Sassoon. But Owen deletes this 'dedication' altogether in a later version to, in effect, universalise the poem. 'Dulce et Decorum Est' is not just about the First World War or 'a Certain Poetess', but about any war and any person who might characterise warfare as glorious.

Owen revised 'Dulce et Decorum Est' along with many of his other famous poems including 'Strange Meeting' and 'Anthem for Doomed Youth' whilst he was on home service between January and July 1918, at Scarborough and Ripon. During this time he began assembling the volume he intended to publish after the War entitled *Disabled and Other Poems*. The draft introduction contains some of the most quoted lines in literature:

> *This book is not about heroes. English poetry is not yet fit to speak of them.*
> *Nor is it about deeds, or lands, nor anything about glory, honour, might, majesty, dominion, or power, except War.*
> *Above all I am not concerned with Poetry.*
> *My subject is War, and the pity of War.*
> *The Poetry is in the pity.*

Owen returned to the Front at Amiens in September 1918 and for his *'conspicuous gallantry and devotion to duty'* during an attack on the Fonsomme Line in October, when he captured a German machine gun and *'scores of prisoners'*, he was recommended for the Military Cross. To his mother he set out his role as a solider and a poet, one that is captured in 'Dulce et Decorum Est':

> *I came out here to help these boys—directly by leading them as well as an officer can; indirectly by watching their sufferings that I may speak of them as well as a pleader can. I have done the first.*

On the 29th of October Owen and his battalion moved into the line west of the Sambre-Oise Canal, and north of the tiny village of Ors. On the 31st of October, he wrote what was to be his last letter to his mother from *'The Smoky Cellar of the Forester's House'*. His vivid description of the *'inmates'* is an affectionate portrait of those with whom he served. He happily reassures Susan:

> *It is a great life. I am more oblivious than alas! yourself, dear Mother, of the ghastly glimmering of the guns outside, & the hollow crashing of the shells.*

The letter ends with some of the most poignant words he ever wrote:

> *Of this I am certain you could not be visited by a band of friends half so fine as surround me here.*

On the morning of the 4th of November, Wilfred Owen was killed attempting to cross the Canal with his battalion of the 2nd Manchesters. The war was over just seven days later.

The arresting and moving images in the pages that follow take us to the heart of Owen's poem. Martin Impey's unique perspective has been enhanced by his careful examination of and engagement with the manuscripts, housed in the British Library in London and the Bodleian Library in Oxford, and reproduced here. With an artist's eye and hands, he has brought Owen's words visually before us through haunting, sometimes grotesque and diabolical figures in a palette of striking colour–splashes of red and black, intense blue, stark monochrome. The terrifying vision of a gas attack, the hideous, blood-curdling effects of this weapon of war on the human body, and the relentless, ghastly memory of the surviving witnesses powerfully confront us. Yet for all their horror, Martin Impey's captivating illustrations are also infused with intense poignancy–with the pity that Owen wanted us to feel, and to remember.

Jane Potter
Oxford Brookes University

thirteen

fourteen

Portrait of Wilfred Owen 5th Manchesters, 1916

fifteen

I am not dissatisfied with my years. Everything has been done in bouts: Bouts of awful labour at Shrewsbury & Bordeaux; bouts of amazing pleasure in the Pyrenees, and play at Craiglockhart; bouts of religion at Dunsden; bouts of horrible danger on the Somme; bouts of poetry always; of your affection always; sympathy for the oppressed always.

I go out of this year a Poet, my dear Mother, as I did not enter it. I am held peer by the Georgians; I am a poet's poet.

I am started. The tugs have left me, I feel the great swelling of the open sea taking my galleon.

Wilfred

Extract from a letter to Susan Owen, New Years Eve, 1917 - Scarborough.

sixteen

Owen's
Original
Manuscripts

Dulce et Decorum est.
(To Jessie Pope etc.)

Bent ~~Hunched~~, like old rag & bone men under sacks;
Knock-kneed, coughing like hags, we cursed through sludge.
Till on the glimmering ~~flares we fall~~ flares we turned our backs,
And towards our distant rest began to trudge.
Halting each mile, ~~*****~~, for some had lost their boots,
And limped on, blood-shod. All went lame; all blind;
Drunk with fatigue; deaf even to the hoots
Of disappointed ~~*****~~ shells that dropped behind.
Then somewhere near in front: Whew, fup, fop, fup —
Gas-shells or duds? We loosened masks in case —
And listened... Nothing... Far guns grumbled ~~Krupp~~ —
Then smartly Poison hit us in the face.
Gas! GAS! An ecstasy of fumbling,
~~*****~~ just in time.
~~*****~~
Fitting the clumsy helmets

P.T.O.

But someone still was yelling out, and stumbling,
And floundering like a man in fire or lime.
There, through the misty panes and dim green light,
As under a thick sea, I saw him drowning...

I must not speak of this thing as I might.
In all my dreams I hear him choking, drowning.
In all your dreams if you could slowly pace
Behind the wagon that we laid him in,
And watch the white eyes turning in his face,
His hanging face, tortured for your own sin,—
If you could see, at every jolt, the blood
Come belching black and frothy from the lung,
And think how once his face was like a bud,
Fresh as a country rose, and clear, and young,
You would not go on telling with such zest,
To children ardent for some desperate glory,
The old lie: Dulce et decorum est

Pro patria mori.

Oct. 8. 1917

Dulce et Decorum est.

~~To Jessie Pope etc.~~ To a certain Poetess.

Bent double, like old beggars under sacks,
Knock-kneed, coughing like hags, we cursed through sludge,
Till on the ~~clawing~~ haunting flares we turned our backs.
And towards our distant rest began to trudge.
Dead slow we moved. Many had lost their boots,
But limped on, blood-shod. All went lame; all blind;
Drunk with fatigue; deaf even to the hoots
~~Of disappointed shells that dropped behind.~~
Of ~~tired-voiced~~ five-nines that dropped behind.
~~두 outstripped~~

Then somewhere near in front: Whew ... fup ... fop ... fup ...
Gas-shells or duds? We loosened masks, in case—
And listened.... Nothing... Far rumouring of Krupp ...
Then ~~smelly~~ stinging poison hit us in the face.
Gas! GAS! — ~~An ecstasy~~ An ecstasy of fumbling.
Quick, boys!
Fitting the clumsy helmets just in time.
But someone still was yelling out, and stumbling,
And floundering like a man in fire or lime.—
Dim, through the misty panes and thick green light,
As under a dark sea, I saw him drowning.

In all my dreams, before my helpless sight,
He plunges at me, ~~gargling~~, choking, drowning.
~~goggling~~
guttering

In all your sobbing dreams, when if you must slowly pace
                                     comes
Behind the limber that we flung him in,
And watch the white eyes turning in his face,   sick
                                          dead of
His hanging face, like a devil's ~~drunk with sin~~,
                can
If ~~your~~ you ~~could~~ hear, at every jolt, the blood
Come gargling black and frothy from the lung,
And think how, once, his face was like a bud,
                                    clean
Fresh as a country rose, and ~~pure~~, and young,—
    'll not repeat   a noble
You ~~would~~ ~~not go on~~ ~~telling~~ with such zest
       small boys
To ~~children~~ ardent for some desperate glory,
    centuries
The ~~old~~ lie : Dulce et decorum est

Pro patria mori.

———

You'd not continue telling
You'd not go telling with such noble zest

Dulce et Decorum est.
[To a certain Poetess]

Bent double, like old beggars under sacks,
Knock-kneed, coughing like hags, we cursed through sludge,
Till on the clawing flares we turned our backs,
And towards our distant rest began to trudge,
Dragging the worst amongst us, who'd no boots
But limped on, blood-shod. All went lame; all blind;
Drunk with fatigue; deaf even to the hoots
Of tired, outstripped five-nines that dropped behind.

Then somewhere near in front: Whew ... fup ... fop ... fup ...
Gas shells or duds? We loosened masks in case —
And listened ... Nothing ... Far rumouring of Krupp ...
Then smartly, poison hit us in the face.
Gas! GAS! Quick boys! — And ecstasy of fumbling,
Fitting the clumsy helmets, just in time.
But someone still was yelling out, and stumbling,
And floundering like a man in fire or lime.

Dim, through the misty panes and heavy light,
As under a dark sea, I saw him drowning.
In all my dreams, before my helpless sight
He lunges at me, guttering, choking, drowning.

In all your dreams if you could slowly pace
Behind the limber that we flung him in,
And watch the white eyes turning in his face,
His hanging face, like a devil's dead of sin;
If you could hear, at every jolt, the blood
Come gargling ~~green~~ thick and frothy from the lung;
And think how once his face was like a bud,
Fresh as a country rose, and ~~bright~~ keen, and young,
You'd not go telling with such noble zest,
To small boys, ardent ~~from~~ for some desperate glory,
The old lie; Dulce et decorum est
Pro patria mori.

      Wilfred Owen.

Dulce et Decorum est.

Bent double, like old beggars under sacks,
Knock-kneed, coughing like hags, we cursed through sludge,
Till on the haunting flares we turned our backs
And towards our distant rest began the trudge.
Men marched asleep. Many had lost their boots
But limped on, blood-shod. All went lame; all blind;
Drunk with fatigue; deaf even to the hoots
Of tired, outstripped Five-Nines that dropped behind.
gas shells dropping softly

Then somewhere near in front: Whew...fup, fop, fup,
Gas shells? Or duds? We loosened masks in case,—
And listened. Nothing. Far rumouring of Krupp.
Then sudden poisons hit us in the face.
Gas! GAS! Quick, boys! — An ecstasy of fumbling,
Fitting the clumsy helmets just in time;
But someone still was yelling out and stumbling,
And flound'ring like a man in fire or lime...
Dim, through the misty panes and thick green light,
As under a green sea, I saw him drowning.

In all my dreams, before my helpless sight,
He plunges at me, guttering, choking, drowning.

In all your dreams, my friend, if you could pace
Behind the wagon that we flung him in,
And watch the white eyes writhing in his face,
His hanging face, like a devil's sick of sin;
If you could hear, at every jolt, the blood
Come gargling from the froth-corrupted lungs
Obscene as 'cancer',
Fresh as a country rose, and keen, and young,—
You'd not repeat with such a noble zest,
To children ardent for some desperate glory,
The old Lie: Dulce et decorum est
Pro patria mori.

Of vile, incurable sores bitter as the cud tongues
My friend, you would not tell with such high zest

To children

Dulce et Decorum Est

Bent double, like old beggars under sacks,
Knock-kneed, coughing like hags, we cursed through sludge,
Till on the haunting flares we turned our backs
And towards our distant rest began to trudge.
Men marched asleep. Many had lost their boots
But limped on, blood-shod. All went lame; all blind;
Drunk with fatigue; deaf even to the hoots
Of tired, outstripped Five-Nines that dropped behind.

Gas! GAS! Quick, boys! – An ecstacy of fumbling,
Fitting the clumsy helmets just in time;
But someone still was yelling out and stumbling,
And flound'ring like a man in fire or lime...
Dim, through the misty panes and thick green light,
As under a green sea, I saw him drowning.

In all my dreams, before my helpless sight,
He plunges at me, guttering, choking, drowning.

If in some smothering dreams you too could pace
Behind the wagon that we flung him in,
And watch the white eyes writhing in his face,
His hanging face, like a devil's sick of sin;
If you could hear, at every jolt, the blood
Come gargling from the froth-corrupted lungs,
Obscene as cancer, bitter as the cud
Of vile, incurable sores on innocent tongues, –
My friend, you would not tell with such high zest
To children ardent for some desperate glory,
The old Lie: Dulce et decorum est
Pro patria mori.

Wilfred Owen

This version of 'Dulce et Decorum Est' is taken from
"Wilfred Owen: The War Poems" (Chatto & Windus, 1994), editor, Jon Stallworthy.

twenty-eight

For those
who will never be old.

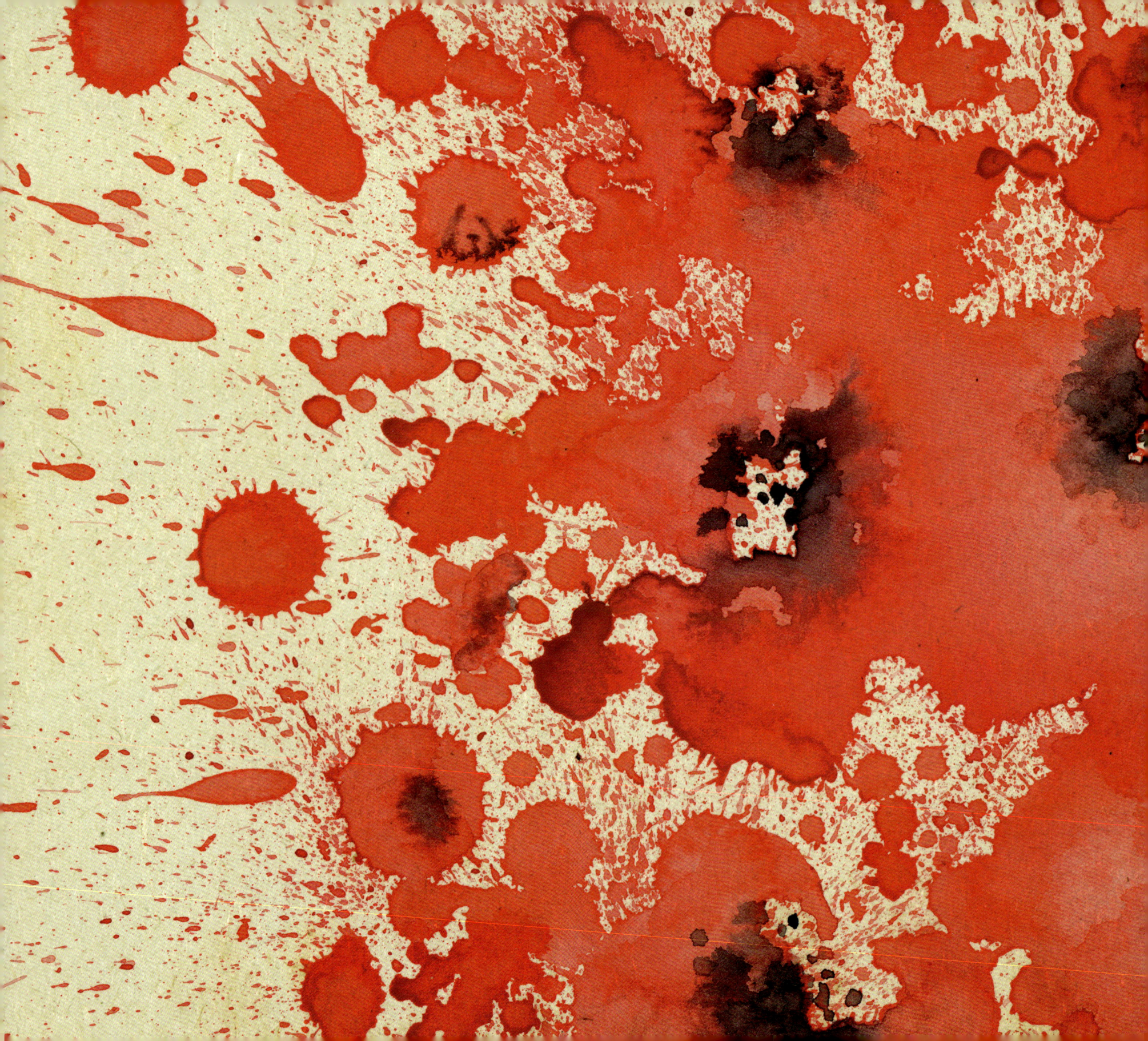

thirty-three

*Bent double,
like old beggars under sacks,*

Hunched

thirty-six

Knock-kneed, coughing like hags,

forty

forty-two

Till on the haunting flares
we turned our backs...

forty-seven

Men marched asleep

Many had lost their boots
But limped on,
blood-shod.
All went lame;

all blind;

Drunk with fatigue;

deaf even to the hoots of tired,

outstripped Five-Nines that dropped behind...

Quick, boys! —

An ecstasy of fumbling,

Fitting the clumsy helmets

just in time;

sixty

But someone still was *yelling out and stumbling,*

And flound'ring like a man in fire or lime...

Dim, through the misty panes and thick green light,

In all my dreams
before my helpless sight
He plunges
at me

guttering
choking
drowning

*If in some smothering dreams
you too could pace
Behind the wagon
that we flung him in,*

seventy-three

And watch
the white eyes
writhing in his face

His
hanging
face,

If you could hear, at every jolt, the blood

Come gargling from the froth-corrupted lungs,

Obscene as cancer,

*bitter as the cud
of vile,
incurable
sores on
innocent
tongues,*

*My friend,
you would not tell
with such
high zest*

eighty-five

small boys
to children
To children ardent for some desperate... glory,

The Old Lie:

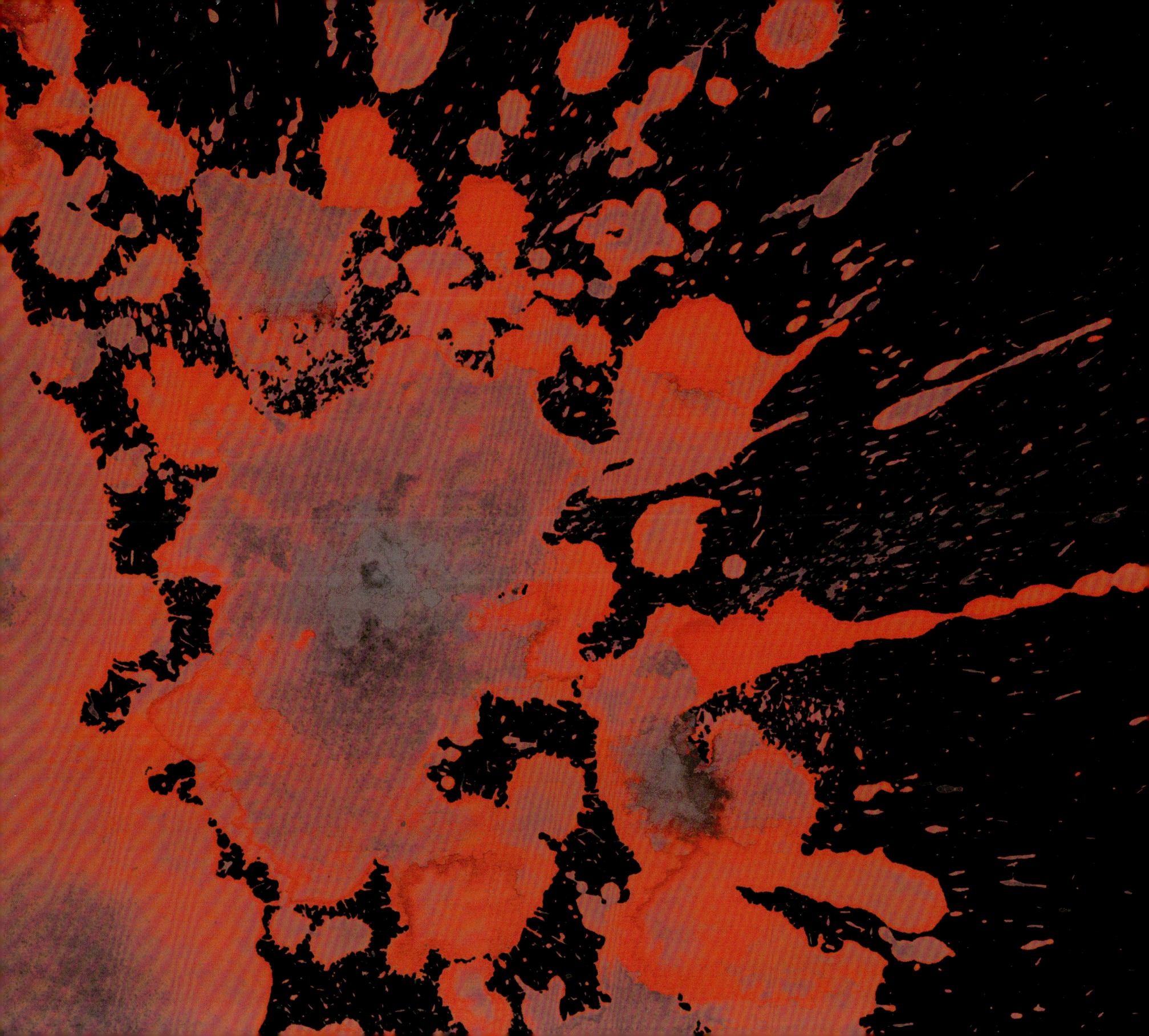

*2nd Lieutenant Wilfred Owen MC was killed in action
on the morning of the 4th November 1918, as the 2nd Manchesters
were attempting to cross the Sambre-Oise canal at Ors France.*

*His mother received the news on 11th November
as bells were ringing out to mark the Armistice.*

'Some say God caught them even before they fell...'

WESO

Thank you

Peter Owen 1940-2018.

Dr Jane Potter, Hilary Robinson, Megan Brownrigg, Lady Lucy French, Maddie Messenger, Robert Baker, Judith Priestman, Oliver House, Samantha Sherbourne, Helen Gilio - Bodleian Library, Oxford, Laura Walker - The British Library, Sian Phillips - Bridgeman Images, Gary Brandham & a special thank you always to Emilie James.

PICTURE CREDITS

The following images are © British Library Board. All Rights Reserved/ Bridgeman Images, reproduced with kind permission of the Trustees of the Wilfred Owen Literary Estate: p.20 & p.21 Add. MS 43721; p.24 Add. MS43720 (f21r); p.25 Add. MS43720 (f22r).

The following images are © The Bodleian Libraries, The University of Oxford, reproduced with kind permission of the Trustees of the Wilfred Owen Literary Estate: Wilfred Owen Archive: p.14 Box 36, 1D; p.18 Fols. 316r; p.19 Fols 317r; p.22 Fols 318r; p.23 Fols 318v; p.92 Box 35, 8(c).

WhereThePoppiesNowGrow

@Martin_Impey

STRAUSS HOUSE
PRODUCTIONS

www.strausshouseproductions.com